FIRST 50 SONGS

YOU SHOULD PLAY ON THE VIOLA

ISBN 978-1-5400-7009-8

Visit Hal Leonard Online at
www.halleonard.com

Contact us:
Hal Leonard
7777 West Bluemound Road
Milwaukee, WI 53213
Email: info@halleonard.com

In Europe, contact:
Hal Leonard Europe Limited
42 Wigmore Street
Marylebone, London, W1U 2RN
Email: info@halleonardeurope.com

In Australia, contact:
Hal Leonard Australia Pty. Ltd.
4 Lentara Court
Cheltenham, Victoria, 3192 Australia
Email: info@halleonard.com.au

ALL OF ME

VIOLA

Words and Music by JOHN STEPHENS
and TOBY GAD

Slowly, in 2

ALL YOU NEED IS LOVE

VIOLA

Words and Music by JOHN LENNON
and PAUL McCARTNEY

AMAZING GRACE

VIOLA

Traditional American Melody

BASIN STREET BLUES

VIOLA

Words and Music by
SPENCER WILLIAMS

(small notes optional)

BEST SONG EVER

VIOLA

Words and Music by EDWARD DREWETT,
WAYNE HECTOR, JULIAN BUNETTA
and JOHN RYAN

CANON IN D

VIOLA

By JOHANN PACHELBEL

Moderately

CARNIVAL OF VENICE

By JULIUS BENEDICT

VIOLA

Moderately, with motion

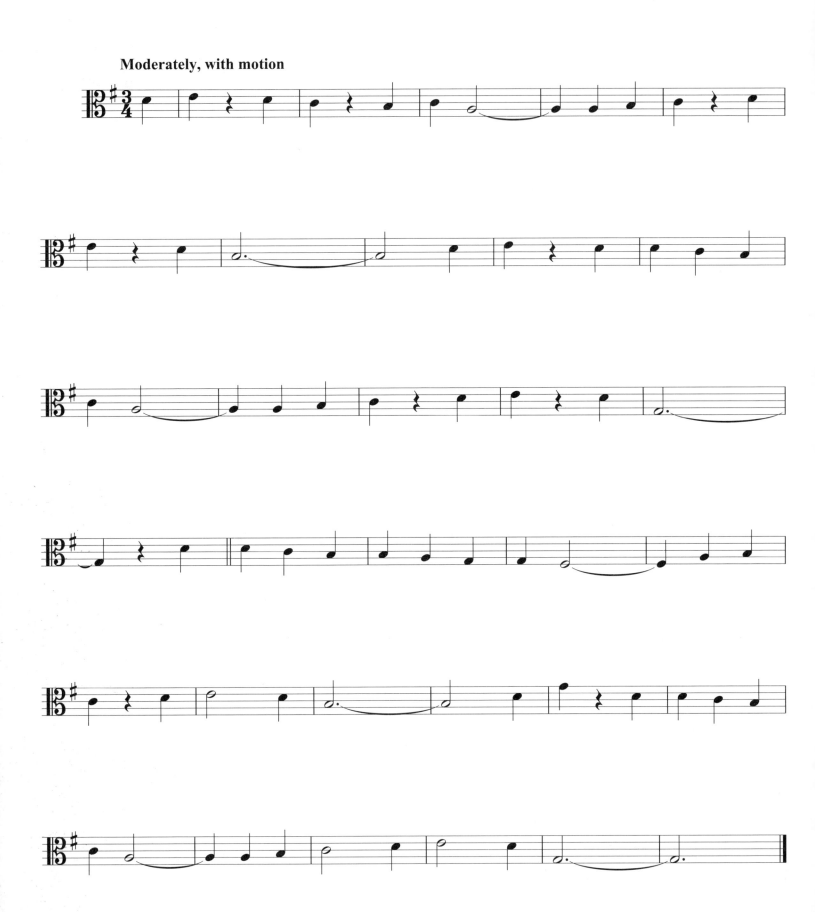

CIRCLE OF LIFE

from THE LION KING

VIOLA

Music by ELTON JOHN
Lyrics by TIM RICE

Moderately (with an African beat)

DUST IN THE WIND

VIOLA

Words and Music by
KERRY LIVGREN

Viola 1

Viola 2

ELEANOR RIGBY

VIOLA

Words and Music by JOHN LENNON
and PAUL McCARTNEY

EVERMORE
from BEAUTY AND THE BEAST

VIOLA

Music by ALAN MENKEN
Lyrics by TIM RICE

FIGHT SONG

VIOLA

Words and Music by RACHEL PLATTEN
and DAVE BASSETT

FLY ME TO THE MOON
(In Other Words)

VIOLA

Words and Music by
BART HOWARD

THE FOOL ON THE HILL

VIOLA

Words and Music by JOHN LENNON
and PAUL McCARTNEY

GOD BLESS AMERICA®

VIOLA

Words and Music by
IRVING BERLIN

Moderately

THE GODFATHER
(Love Theme)
from the Paramount Picture THE GODFATHER

VIOLA

By NINO ROTA

Slowly and expressively

HALLELUJAH

VIOLA

Words and Music by
LEONARD COHEN

Moderately slow, in 2

HAPPY
from DESPICABLE ME 2

VIOLA

Words and Music by
PHARRELL WILLIAMS

HELLO

VIOLA

Words and Music by
LIONEL RICHIE

Slow Ballad

HELLO, DOLLY!

from HELLO, DOLLY!

VIOLA

Music and Lyric by
JERRY HERMAN

Medium Strut

HOW DEEP IS YOUR LOVE
from the Motion Picture SATURDAY NIGHT FEVER

VIOLA

Words and Music by BARRY GIBB,
ROBIN GIBB and MAURICE GIBB

Moderately

THE HUSTLE

VIOLA

Words and Music by
VAN McCOY

Moderately

I WILL ALWAYS LOVE YOU

VIOLA

Words and Music by
DOLLY PARTON

Moderately slow

(small note optional)

JESU, JOY OF MAN'S DESIRING

VIOLA

English Words by ROBERT BRIDGES
Music by JOHANN SEBASTIAN BACH

THE IRISH WASHERWOMAN

VIOLA

Irish Folksong

JUST GIVE ME A REASON

VIOLA

Words and Music by ALECIA MOORE,
JEFF BHASKER and NATE RUESS

CODA

JUST THE WAY YOU ARE

VIOLA

Words and Music by BRUNO MARS,
ARI LEVINE, PHILIP LAWRENCE,
KHARI CAIN and KHALIL WALTON

To Coda $\oplus$ Fine

D.S. al Coda   CODA $\oplus$

D.S. al Fine

LET IT GO
from FROZEN

VIOLA

Music and Lyrics by KRISTEN ANDERSON-LOPEZ
and ROBERT LOPEZ

Fine

D.S. al Fine

MAS QUE NADA

VIOLA

Words and Music by
JORGE BEN

MY HEART WILL GO ON
(Love Theme from 'Titanic')
from the Paramount and Twentieth Century Fox Motion Picture TITANIC

VIOLA

Music by JAMES HORNER
Lyric by WILL JENNINGS

NIGHT TRAIN

VIOLA

Words by OSCAR WASHINGTON
and LEWIS C. SIMPKINS
Music by JIMMY FORREST

PERFECT

VIOLA

Words and Music by
ED SHEERAN

PURE IMAGINATION
from WILLY WONKA AND THE CHOCOLATE FACTORY

VIOLA

Words and Music by LESLIE BRICUSSE
and ANTHONY NEWLEY

ROAR

VIOLA

Words and Music by KATY PERRY,
MAX MARTIN, DR. LUKE,
BONNIE McKEE and HENRY WALTER

Moderately

ROLLING IN THE DEEP

VIOLA

Words and Music by ADELE ADKINS
and PAUL EPWORTH

SATIN DOLL

VIOLA

By DUKE ELLINGTON

THEME FROM "SCHINDLER'S LIST"

from the Universal Motion Picture SCHINDLER'S LIST

VIOLA

Music by JOHN WILLIAMS

SEE YOU AGAIN

from FURIOUS 7

Viola

Words and Music by CAMERON THOMAZ,
CHARLIE PUTH, JUSTIN FRANKS,
ANDREW CEDAR, DANN HUME,
JOSH HARDY and PHOEBE COCKBURN

SHAKE IT OFF

VIOLA

Words and Music by TAYLOR SWIFT,
MAX MARTIN and SHELLBACK

STAND BY ME

VIOLA

Words and Music by JERRY LEIBER,
MIKE STOLLER and BEN E. KING

Moderately, with a beat

THE STAR-SPANGLED BANNER

VIOLA

Words by FRANCIS SCOTT KEY
Music by JOHN STAFFORD SMITH

With spirit

STAY WITH ME

VIOLA

Words and Music by SAM SMITH,
JAMES NAPIER, WILLIAM EDWARD PHILLIPS,
TOM PETTY and JEFF LYNNE

STOMPIN' AT THE SAVOY

VIOLA

By BENNY GOODMAN,
EDGAR SAMPSON and CHICK WEBB

Bright Swing

SUMMERTIME
from PORGY AND BESS®

VIOLA

Music and Lyrics by GEORGE GERSHWIN,
DuBOSE and DOROTHY HEYWARD
and IRA GERSHWIN

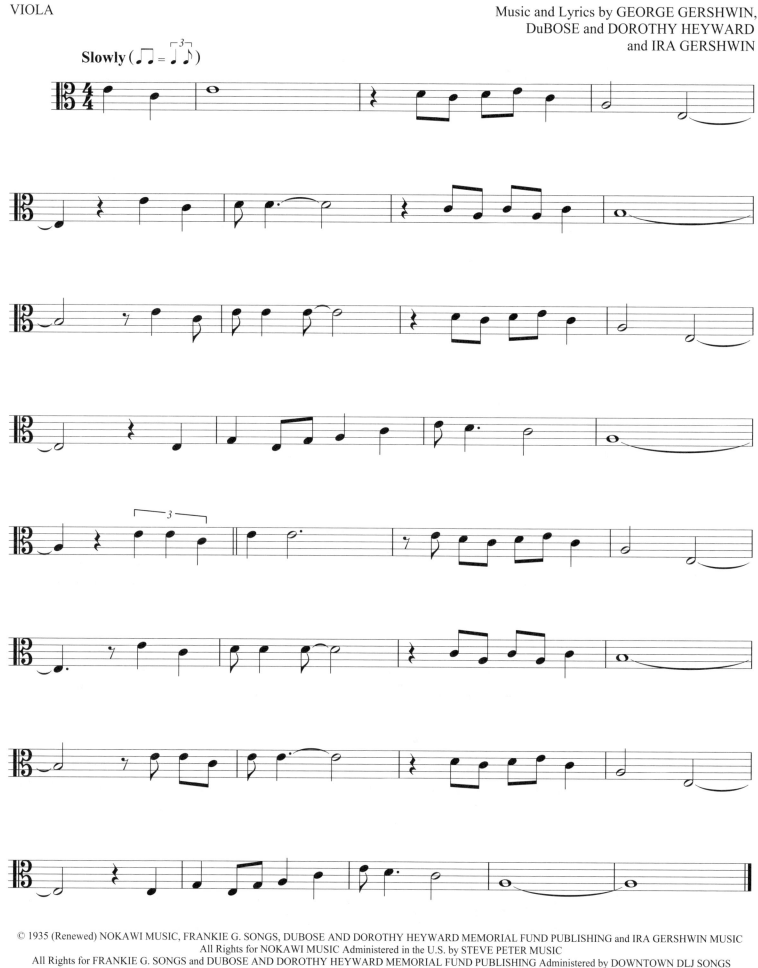

TENNESSEE WALTZ

VIOLA

Words and Music by REDD STEWART
and PEE WEE KING

TURKEY IN THE STRAW

VIOLA

American Folksong

Moderately, in 2

THIS IS ME
from THE GREATEST SHOWMAN

VIOLA

Words and Music by BENJ PASEK
and JUSTIN PAUL

UPTOWN FUNK

VIOLA

Words and Music by MARK RONSON,
BRUNO MARS, PHILIP LAWRENCE, JEFF BHASKER, DEVON GALLASPY,
NICHOLAUS WILLIAMS, LONNIE SIMMONS, RONNIE WILSON,
CHARLES WILSON, RUDOLPH TAYLOR and ROBERT WILSON

VIVA LA VIDA

VIOLA

Words and Music by GUY BERRYMAN,
JON BUCKLAND, WILL CHAMPION
and CHRIS MARTIN

YOU RAISE ME UP

VIOLA

Words and Music by BRENDAN GRAHAM
and ROLF LOVLAND

Moderately slow

small notes optional